w

Bernd Desinger

Unhadronische Materie
Rocklyrik und Gedichte

Unhadronic Matter
Rocklyrics and Poems

Vorwort von / Introduction by
Ranga Yogeshwar

Wiesenburg Verlag

Bibliographische Information Der Deutschen Nationalbibliothek:
Die Deutsche Nationalbibliothek verzeichnet diese Publikation
in der Deutschen Nationalbibliographie;
detaillierte bibliographische Daten sind im Internet
über http://dnb.ddb.de abrufbar.

1. Auflage 2006
Wiesenburg Verlag
Postfach 4410, 97412 Schweinfurt
www.wiesenburgverlag.de
Alle Rechte beim Verlag
Cover-Entwurf: Dipl.-Grafikerin Susanne Renner-Desinger
Druckorganisation: A2 die Agentur, Seeweg 12, 96164 Kemmern

ISBN 3-939518-12-3

Vorwort

In den Tiefen des Universums provozieren Ungereimtheiten unser derzeitiges Weltbild: Die Umlaufgeschwindigkeiten von Sternen in Spiralgalaxien lassen sich nicht mit der bekannten sichtbaren Materie erklären. Auch die Bewegung von Kugelsternhaufen, die Dynamik von Galaxienhaufen oder die Expansion des Universums zwingen die Kosmologie, die bisher angenommene Materiezusammensetzung im Weltraum zu überdenken.

In den vielfältigen Erklärungsversuchen der Astrophysik spekuliert man sogar, daß unser Kosmos überwiegend aus völlig unbekannter "Dunkler Materie" und "Dunkler Energie" bestehen könnte. Demnach würde die uns bekannte hadronische Materie nur einen Bruchteil ausmachen.

Die Existenz einer "Unhadronischen Materie" anzunehmen mag frustrierend sein im Hinblick auf unsere Naturgesetze und Ordnungssysteme, jedoch eröffnet sie unserer Phantasie ganz neue Dimensionen!

Auch die Liedertexte und Gedichte, die Bernd Desinger unter diesem Titel zusammengestellt hat, entziehen sich einer Einordnung in bekannte Kategorien. In großer stilistischer und inhaltlicher Bandbreite spiegeln die von 1985 bis 2005 entstandenen Texte dieser "Best of"-Kompilation auch das Leben des Autors in und zwischen Deutschland, Europa und Nordamerika wider.

Die Texte stammen unter anderem aus den Zyklen "Gesänge der See", "Aufzeichnungen eines Verstörten", "Age of Angst", "Feast or Famine", "Kaltstart", "The Black T-Shirt" und "Nächtliche Begegnungen" sowie aus dem Programm der Artrock-Band "design".
Wiedergegeben ist jeweils die deutsche oder englische Originalversion der Texte.

Ranga Yogeshwar

Introduction

Inconsistencies in the depth of the universe challenge our current worldview: the orbital velocity of stars in spiral galaxies cannot be explained by known visible matter. The movement of globular clusters, the dynamics of galaxy clusters, and the expansion of the universe force the cosmologist to re-evaluate the composition of space.

Astrophysicists speculate that a major part of our cosmos consists of as yet unknown "Dark Energy" and "Dark Matter". Hence, current known hadronic matter is only a small part of the entire cosmos.

Assuming the existence of "Unhadronic Matter" frustrates our current understanding of the laws of nature and other classification systems, yet such an assumption opens new dimensions for our imagination!

The lyrics and poems compiled by Bernd Desinger under this title do not fit into usual categories either. With a broad variety in both style and content, the texts of this "Best of" collection, written between 1985 and 2005, reflect the author's life in and between Germany, Europe and North America.

The lyrics and poems are taken from -among others- the cycles "Gesänge der See", "Aufzeichnungen eines Verstörten", "Age of Angst", "Feast or Famine", "Kaltstart", "The Black T-Shirt" and "Nächtliche Begegnungen", as well as from the concert program of the Artrockband "design". The texts are each presented in their German or English original version.

Ranga Yogeshwar

Inhaltsverzeichnis/Table of Contents:
aus/from:

Gesänge der See (1986)
Da war ein Regen	13
Gesänge der See	14
Y-sevys war'n carrygy	15
Portquin	16
Nun dreht sich der Wind	17

Aufzeichnungen eines Verstörten (1985)
Der moralisierende Präzeptor und sein Schiff fröhlicher Narren	18
Gesichter	19
Zufall	20
Jemand spielt Saxophon	21
Der fliegende Robert	25

Vermischtes (1986)
Die andere Seite	26
Ein Flugzeug	27
Ischariot's Alraune	28
The Space Shuttle	30
Die Mühle	31
호수 Der See	32
Spüren	34

Elegies from Athens and Elsewhere (1993)
Ich war nicht in Arkadien geboren	36
Athener Elegie	37
He	38
Two dead Foxes	40
Kap der Bösen Hoffnung	42

Design (1989)
Tschionatulander und Sigune	43
Wie die Schraube entsteht	44
Echofisch	46
Die Brücke und der Fluß	48
Im warmen Wasserturm	49

Reframing (1994)
Frequent Fliers	50
Up there	52

Age of Angst (1995)
Age of Angst	53
Shunting Engine	54
Let go	56
Religious Frenzy	58
Racist Frenzy	60
Twenty-two Black Stretch-Limousines	63
Little Figure Skater	64
Long Shadows	66
Coroner's Car	68
Addicted	70
Mobile Society	72
Virtual Reality	73
Moving on	74

Feast or Famine (1995)
Intolerance	76
You don't love me anymore	79
African-American Girl	80
Feast or Famine	82
Just had to	86
Anxiety Attack	88
Verge of Collapse	90

We're ready when you are (1998)
Ready when you are   92

Kaltstart (2001)
Mein Schmerz und Ich   94
Strg + Alt + Entf   96
Mit Dir und in Dir   98
Andere   99
Mein Wissen ist nur angelesen   100

The Black T-Shirt (2004)
The Black T-Shirt   101
When you ain't got a friend   104
Cold Spring Rain   106

Nächtliche Begegnungen (2005)
Ich dringe in Dich   107
Fasan   108
Ex und Hopp   110
Kleiner Pilot   112
Wolkengesicht   113
Lichtgestalt   114
Sternschnuppe   116
Feuergeist   118

Acknowledgement/Danksagung:

"Y-sevys war'n carrygy" - Übertragung ins
cornische Keltisch/Translation into Cornish Celtic:
P. A. S. Pool, Penzance/Cornwall (1986)
"호 수" Übertragung ins Koreanische/
Translation into Korean:
Eomki Sung, Seoul (1992)
Young Lee, Los Angeles (2006)

Da war ein Regen

Da war ein Regen, war ein Sturm
Er ist ins Feld geschlagen
Er mähte die Ähren vor dem Schnitter

Leicht zittert die Luft noch
Doch die Wolken stehn jetzt fester
Auf den Hügeln am Horizont

Eine Möwe schwebt durch die Senke
Durch die Wipfel der Bäume
Deren Blätter fremde Sprachen sprechen
Ich komme etwas näher

Gesänge der See

Aus dem Hafen, aus der Bucht
Das Gelächter dringt herauf zu den Klippen
Seeleute singen Gesänge der See
Ein Schemen von Licht überm Wasser schwebt

Klar die Sterne, hart rollt das Meer
Am Ende des Bogens flackern die Fackeln
Und unter den Schwingen der Möwen drehn
Sich dunkel die Winde der Nacht

Y-sevys war'n carrygy

Y-sevys war'n carrygy
Dhe dheweth termyn
Rag un pols
Kemyskys en
Gans an gwyns
An comolow
H'an
Mor pell glas

                Ich stand auf den Felsen
                Am Ende der Zeit
                Für einen Augenblick
                War ich eins
                Mit dem Wind
                Den Wolken
                Und
                Der weiten, blauen See

Portquin

Seven sailors sailed for fishing
For fishing the whiting
Off of the shore and out to the sea
The deep smooth sea
For fishing the whiting
Out to the sea
And then so sudden
The force of the storm
Screwed the seven
To the heart of the ocean
They never reshored
And the women cried
But not for long
They all left
The empty beach of Portquin

Nun dreht sich der Wind

Nun dreht sich der Wind
Und trägt etwas mehr herüber
Von den Klängen der Blaskapelle
Welche mit dem Tosen der Welle
Kämpft und doch nicht siegt

Das Meer zerschlägt sich
Seinen Kopf an Zackenfelsen
Dabei spritzt es weiß
Das Blaugrün kocht heiß
In ewigem Todeskampf

**Der moralisierende Präzeptor
und sein Schiff fröhlicher Narren**

Jetzt ist wieder Karneval
Ach, was haben wir gelacht
Ich sah einen Kapitän
Er steuerte sein Narrenschiff
Mit verbundnen Augen
Fröhlich in die Schlacht

Gelassen, gelassen, Gelassenheit
Rief er vom Ruder herab
Die Menge johlte vor Begeisterung
Taumelte trunken auf den Planken
Als gäbe es kein nasses Grab

Jetzt ist wieder Karneval
Ach, was haben wir gelacht
Der Lindwurm walzte
Durch die Straßen der Stadt
Hinter den Lippen grinste die Macht

Am Aschermittwoch klebte kalt
Bier auf Bürgersteigen
Nur Schneereste, konfettibunt
Zeugten von der lustigen Fahrt

Jemand raunte ein Schiff sei untergegangen
Doch niemand wußte wo
Es abgeblieben war

Jetzt ist wieder Karneval
Ach, was haben wir gelacht
Ach, was haben wir gelacht

Gesichter

Gestern malte ich
Mein Gesicht an
Die eine Hälfte tiefrot
Die andere tiefgrün
Und meine Augen schwarz
Eine junge Frau erschrak
Als blickte sie in einen Spiegel
Eine Mutter drehte sich
Mit ihren Kindern um
Ein weißer Malermeister
Musterte mich stumm
Ein Punk hob die Bierflasche
Mir zum Gruß
Und radelte vorbei
Der Briefträger lächelte freundlich
Der Müllmann sah
Verlegen drein
Ein Rentner hob zur Abwehr
Seinen Stock
Am Spielplatz hob ein Hund
Sein Bein
Modische Schulmädchen
Kicherten heimlich
Und eine Oma
Suchte auf meiner Stirn
Die Zahl des Tieres

Ich glaube
Die meisten
Hielten mich wohl
Für einen
Spinner

Zufall

Ich traf Dich wieder
Ganz plötzlich durch Zufall
Alles war anders
Du warst nicht mehr Du

In Deinen Augen
War nunmehr kein Glänzen
Der Hauch des Schweigens
Schloß mir den Hals zu

Ich dachte, da wäre nichts mehr
Doch ich hatte noch etwas
Ich dachte, da gäbe es nichts mehr

Doch da war noch etwas
An das ich nicht glaubte
Weil ich es nicht sah

Jemand spielt Saxophon

Als der Wind sich drehte
Wollte ich kein Fähnchen sein
Wollte von offenen Himmeln aufgesogen werden

Warum irre ich durch Labyrinthe
Wirbel im Strom der Ventilatoren?
Alles, was ich berühre, weicht zurück
Alles, was ich halten will
Wird zu Sand
Ich seh' ihn durch meine Finger rinnen
Irgendwo im Dunst verfließen

Trommeln schlagen
Feuer in der Nacht
Ich schreie und strecke meine Hände in die Leere
Boten des Schreckens drohen in den Wolken – Gefahr

Hoch im verschneiten Bergdorf
Versucht vergeblich ein kleiner Junge
Vor dem Schneepflug zu fliehen -
Überrollt und zerquetscht
Später stoppt er mit ausgebreiteten Armen
Rote Schienenbusse auf gerodeten Waldhängen

Ganz deutlich höre ich jetzt Sätze und Wörter
Sehe Gesichter, die ich nicht kenne
Jahre danach kommt dieser Augenblick
Zwischen Magiern und Schamanen
Wiederholt sich das alles
Frage ich den einen Seelenarzt
Frage die Frage
Antwort die Antwort
Die ich so gut kenne

Jemand spielt Saxophon

Mein Gesicht wird zu Stein
Der Psychiater schreit
Was ist? Wo bist du?
Hörst du nicht? Was bist du?
Kennst du nicht?
Ich sage: Jemand spielt Saxophon

Türen fallen in Schlösser
Und der Kaffee ist fertig
Doch da ist Satz auf dem Boden
Ich schüttle mich
Kann nicht lesen
Und kann nicht spucken

In der Ecke steht ein nacktes Mädchen
Habe ich ihr Gesicht nicht schon gesehen?
Wollten ihre Augen nicht auf vollen Weiden wandern?
Ich will sie fragen

Die Tasse entgleitet mir und zerschlägt auf dem Boden
Nein! schreit sie, nicht zu nahe
Vorsicht, der Bannkreis
Du wirst verglühen
Doch sie zieht zwischen ihren Beinen wie zum Trost
Einen Terminkalender hervor
Und reicht ihn mir herüber
Funken sprühen
Ich blättere in den Seiten
Und lese in Sekunden
Millionen von Daten
Millionen von Namen
Meiner ist nicht darunter
Als ich ihr den Terminkalender
Zurückgeben will
Ist sie verschwunden
Achtlos werfe ich ihn fort

Draußen scheint es noch immer zu regnen
Der Schamane spielt mit Ketten
Ich suche meinen Bruder
Angst? Ja, vielleicht
Im Spiegel sehe ich mein Gesicht älter werden
Schnell, es verfällt
Die Bartstoppeln werden grau
Auch meine Lederjacke ist abgewetzt
Die Hosen zerschlissen
Ein Teil von mir stirbt
Ich bin ruhig und warte
Blick aus dem Fenster
Die Leute hasten durch die Straßen
Ich sehe sie
Sie mich nicht.
Fein, denke ich
Plötzlich fällt die Jalousie

Im Dunkeln bekomme ich Angst
Doch der Schamane summt
Und es geht mir besser
Ein Wind tut sich auf
Und es riecht nach Meer
Nach kalten Klippen
Und einsamen Vögeln
Die Fensterläden knarren
Ich lege mich hin
Und schließe die Augen
Eine warme Hand
Der Magier lacht
Unheimlich durch den Sturm
Irgendwo fahles Mondlicht
Ein schwarzer Rabe
Läßt sich mit ausgebreiteten Schwingen
Auf der Schulter des Schamanen nieder

Etwas tropft von der Wand
Ich tauche meinen Finger
In das Rinnsal
Es schmeckt wie Blut
Da beginnt mein Finger zu leuchten
Das Glimmen breitet sich aus
Bald leuchtet die ganze Hand
Dann der Arm
Bis mein ganzer Körper flimmert
Als die Fußsohlen erfaßt sind
Löst sich mein Körper vom Boden
Ich schwebe

Mit einem Mal scheinen die Wände fort zu sein
Auch der Schamane ist nirgendswo mehr zu sehen
Endlich merke ich
Daß das Schwarz, in welchem ich schwebe
Sich in einen Purpurton verwandelt hat
Ich treibe nacheinander durch verschiedene Farben
Grün
Blau
Gelb
Rot
Ich finde mich in einem naßkalten Herbstwald wieder
Hunde bellen
Fletschen Zähne
Jagdhörner schmettern
Pferdegetrappel
Die Meute scheint näher zu kommen
Im Nebel kann ich nichts erkennen

Der fliegende Robert

Flieg, Robert, flieg!
Hör' nicht auf das, was die andern sagen
Warum will man Dir denn das Fliegen verbieten
Sie haben nur Angst, daß Du mehr kannst als sie

Flieg, Robert, flieg!
Laß' Dir nicht die Flügel stutzen
So stark wie Du bist stürzt Du niemals ab
Der Wind, er wird Dich weitertragen
In eine Welt, die Dir besser gefällt
Der Schirm, er trug Dich sicher herauf
Er bringt Dich irgendwo auch herab

Sie sagen, es ist die Angst um Dich
Doch ihre Augen strotzen vor Neid
Wenn sie Dir über Wolkentürmen folgen
So flieg, Robert, flieg!
Beachte nicht das hohle Geschrei
Sieh nur, es kommt her von unter Dir
Und höre nur, je höher Du bist
Wie unklar das Gejohle ist
Klingt das "Bleib' doch hier!" nicht wie
Ein "Bitte, bitte, nimm' mich mit"?

Flieg!
Flieg!

Die andere Seite

Ich lief durch diesen leeren Steinbruch
Und stand auf einmal am Abgrund
Diesen tiefen Graben zu überwinden
War mein Denken
War mein Fühlen
War ich

Es blieb nur der Weg durch den Urwald
So schwer und fern lag er vor mir
Diesen tiefen Graben zu überwinden
War mein Denken
War mein Fühlen
War ich

Es blieb nur der Weg unterm Wasserfall
Den trocken ich zu kreuzen glaubte
Diesen tiefen Graben zu überwinden
War mein Denken
War mein Fühlen
War ich

Unter der Mitte drehte der Wind
Ich wurde naß
Meine Haare
Mein Rücken
Meine Hose
Meine Schuhe
Aber die andere Seite
Hätte ich erreichen können

Ein Flugzeug

Ist das ein Flugzeug, was ich seh'?
Es kreist am hohen Himmel
Es sägt sich durch den klaren See
Warum flieg' ich nicht mit?

Mich in dieser Sauerstofflanze
Eine Handbreit unterm Mond vorbei
Durch den blauen Stahl zu glühen…
Einen kleinen Augenblick
Würd' ich dann vielleicht glauben
Ich sei frei

Und alles, was noch von mir bliebe
Wär' ein leuchtender Kondensstrahl
Den die Winde bald zerstöben…
Einen kleinen Augenblick
Würdest du vielleicht glauben
Ich sei frei

Ist das ein Flugzeug, was ich seh'?
Es kreist am hohen Himmel
Es sägt sich durch den klaren See
Und ich, ich flieg' nicht mit

Ischariot's Alraune

Aus dem Samen des Gehenkten
Gebar die Erde die Alraune
Ich fand sie am Fuße des Galgens
In einer schwarzblauen Nacht
Starrsilbrig fuhr der Mond durch die Windstille

Unten im Dorf die Alte raunte
Sie trägt dein Gesicht, dein Gesicht
Siehst du, wie die Vögel fliegen
Das bringt kein Glück, kein Glück

Bevor der Hahn dreimal kräht
Werde ich dich verraten haben
Bevor die Sonne untergeht
Habe ich dich verkauft

Ich bin unsicher, so sag' mir doch
Ob ich die Schuld dafür trage
Es wurde doch so prophezeit
Es stand doch so geschrieben
Ich habe nur das Wort erfüllt
Nichts sonst hat mich getrieben

Wehrlos in fremden Plänen verstrickt
War ich ohne Willen ein Werkzeug
Zähe Zangen zogen die Fäden
Starke Strudel sogen mich auf
Mir fehlte die Kraft eines Luzifer
So bin ich unten geblieben

Was wäre Jesus ohne mich
Warum bin ich kein Heiliger?

Unten im Dorf die Alte raunte
Sie trägt dein Gesicht, dein Gesicht
Siehst du, wie die Vögel fliegen
Das bringt kein Glück, kein Glück

Bevor der Hahn dreimal kräht
Werde ich dich verraten haben
Bevor die Sonne untergeht
Habe ich dich verkauft

The Space Shuttle

They shuttle the space the space they shuttle
The space shuttle the shuttle space
They space the space
They shuttle the shuttle
They shuttle the dream

They shuttle the eagle
They shuttle the money
They shuttle the hunger
They shuttle the tears
They say it's a dream
They sell it's a dream
They sell this dream
The dream, the eagle, the money
The dream blew up into the air

The dream grew up to become a fireball
They sell the celluloid
They sell the fireball
They sell the cells of celluloid
And God does bless the celluloid

Die Mühle

Schwarz erhebt sich auf dem Hügel die Mühle
Sie droht mit ihren Flügeln dem Wanderer im Tal
Mahlt mit ihren Steinen das Korn des Lebens zu Mehl
Wanderer, sei willkommen

Dunkle Ozeane saugen das Licht des Tages in sich ein
Die Gesänge der Sirenen schmelzen das Wachs
In des Seemanns Ohr
Über versunkenen Stätten schüttelt Poseidon
Seinen Dreizack
Seemann, sei willkommen

Schwarz erhebt sich auf dem Hügel die Mühle
Sie droht mit ihren Flügeln dem Wanderer im Tal
Mahlt mit ihren Steinen das Korn des Lebens zu Mehl
Wanderer, sei willkommen

호수 Der See

작은 나무 다리가
호수에 있는 조그마한 섬까지 이어져 있네
비에 젖은 산등성이에서
노년의 한 남자와 여자가 차를 마시고
지금은 그 다리에 서서
거울처럼 잔잔한 호수처럼
평온한 숨을 쉬고 있네

온화한 햇살속에서는
날개짓하는 새들의 깃털들
무성한 수풀속에서 자유롭게
찬란한 색으로 빛나고

부드러운 바람결에 출렁이는 갈대들
그 주위를 맴도는 잠자리들
빛은 조각이 되어 퍼지고
무지개
날아다니는 파리들
집을 짓는 거미들
소리들은 잘 어울려져서
늘 그렇게
그리고또 다시
또 늘 그렇게
거울같이 잔잔한 호수처럼
평온한 숨을 쉬고 있네

Aus leichtem Holz eine Brücke
Zur kleinen Insel im See gespannt
Alter Mann und alte Frau tranken Tee
Von den Hängen der Regenberge
Stehend auf der Brücke jetzt
Atem ruhig wie der Spiegel des Sees

In milder Sonne glänzt bunt
Das Gefieder der schwirrenden
In feuchtem Dickicht
Freien Vögel

Schilf wiegend in sanfter Brise
Umschraubt von Libellen
Licht bricht
Regenbögen
Fliegen fliegen
Spinnen spinnen
Stimmen stimmen
Immer
Und wieder
Und immer wieder
Atem ruhig wie der Spiegel des Sees

Spüren

Plötzlich habe ich das Gefühl
Meine Arme um dich legen zu müssen
Es ist so ein Kribbeln in meinen Adern
Ich weiß nicht, wie ich das nennen soll
Ist das Sympathie, wie man sagt, die ich empfinde
Oder ist das mehr, ich weiß es nicht
Vielleicht will ich es auch gar nicht wissen
Vielleicht will ich nur spürn'
Das Gehirn ausschalten, bloß nicht mehr denken
Bloß nah bei dir sein, bloß dich berührn'

Doch die Hände bleiben zur Faust verkrampft
Schwer in den Taschen liegen
Ich quäle mir ein Lächeln heraus
Und frage, ob du noch etwas Tee willst
Du nickst, ich steh' auf und komm' mir blöd vor
Wie ich den Tee eingieße
Was ist das, was hält mich zurück
Hält mich zurück davor dir zu zeigen
Wie sehr ich dich mag
Ich würde diese Mauern niederreißen
Wenn ich nur wüßte wie
Das Gehirn ausschalten, bloß nicht mehr denken
Bloß nah bei dir sein, bloß dich berührn'

Warum fehlt mir der Mut, warum fehlt die Kraft
Einfach das zu tun, was ich will
Nicht mehr reden, ich will' alles vergessen
Nicht mehr abwägen, zaudern, zögern
Einfach handeln, einfach tun

Dann sagst du, es wird Zeit, du mußt jetzt gehn'
Du fandest es nett bei mir
Mit einem leisen Auf Wiedersehen
Bringe ich dich dann zur Tür
Von meinem Fenster aus sehe ich noch
Wie du auf deinem Rad
Langsam um die Ecke biegst

Ich war nicht in Arkadien geboren

Ob auf dichtbelebten Straßen, ob im stillen, hehren Hain
Ob am rauschenden Gestade, immerzu bin ich allein
Steige ich in schwarze Städte, steige ich auf lichte Höhn
Schwirre ich in wilden Strudeln, immerzu bin ich allein

Ich war nicht in Arkadien geboren
An meiner Wiege hat mir keiner Freude zugeschworen
Und Tränen bringt der lange Herbst mir nur

Doch ob schon einsam, so bin ich ganz verloren nicht
Und hab' ich nichts auf dieser grauen Welt
Dann hab' ich immerhin noch Dich

So schwebt Dein Bild hier vor mir
Und das bei jedem Schritt
Und wenn die Sterne untergehen
Ist es ein Licht, das nicht erlischt
Es gibt mir Kraft im Dunkeln, auf dem langen Ritt

Athener Elegie

Wie durch einen Schleier von Gaze hauchdünn
Seh' ich von fern und doch so nah
Dein himmlisches Gesicht
Deine Augen und dein Lächeln
Sind so schön wie nie

Die Strahlung ist so mild
Ein Ton von warmem Blond
Dabei unsagbar traurig
Ist dies wohl ein Zusammenhang
Seltsame Harmonie?

Wird denn erst die Schönheit
Vollkommen durch den Schmerz?
Dein himmlisches Gesicht
Die tosende Brandung in meiner Brust
Ist so stark wie nie

Ein Bild steht vor mir auf dem Tisch
Ich weiß, du kennst sie selber nicht
Die Spurn auf dem Gesicht
Lang pflügt der Landmann auf dem Feld
Die Spurn gehn tief wie nie

Klebrig kriecht der Sand der Zeit auf den Felsen hin
Doch ganz nah ist der Boden schon
Der Himmel, er klart auf
Deine Augen und dein Lächeln
Sanfte Melancholie

Wie durch einen Schleier von Gaze hauchdünn
Seh' ich von fern und doch so nah
Dein himmlisches Gesicht
Deine Augen und dein Lächeln
Sind so schön wie nie

He

It was truly clear
There were no questions
She loved him deeply
Deeper than a river
Or even a sea

She gave him signs
Through her tiny glasses
But he did not realize
For maybe he didn't like dogs
But she loved them

And then one day
She heard of a party
And that he would be there
So she went off leaving her home
Leaving her friends, leaving their doubts
All behind
She went for him
She came along the long, long road

It wasn't he wasn't there
It wasn't she couldn't speak to him
It wasn't she meant nothing to him

She came in vain
She came for nothing
The long, long road
The hills up and down
Just to see him
Just to meet him
She came in vain

It wasn't he hadn't at least
For a moment the thought
Of getting closer
But honest he was
For he knew coming closer
Meant body-talk only
Honest he was
He smiled and then turned
She stood there
And cried
But only inside
The tears had already dried
Before they met her eyes
She came in vain

Two dead Foxes

Two dead foxes
Lying on the shoulder
Head to the road
Lying side by side

Wide open eyes
Neither with questions
Nor with surprise
Maybe just a trace of sadness

Where did they come from
And why did they come?
Apparently they had an aim
Apparently they show disdain

With their proud broken eyes
They blame us the questioners
Asking us where our highway leads to
Accusing

Two dead foxes
Coming from nowhere
Like me and you
Where does our highway lead?

We're so frightened
Two without hope
Head to the road
We ain't got the heart of foxes

You don't have no questions
In your eyes there's just sadness
We go down on our knees
Our hearts are trembling

We don't have no strength

Two dead foxes
Lying on the shoulder
Head to the road
Lying side by side

Kap der Bösen Hoffnung

Ich steh' an meinem Fenster
Und schau' hinaus in die Nacht
Von fern hör' ich die Gleise raunen
Es ist die Zeit zum Träumen

Und dann geh' ich hinaus
Übers weite Feld
Der Himmel so klar
Und so kalt die Nacht

Jetzt steh' ich fast am Gleis
Und ich spür' ein Zittern
Dann dröhnt der Boden
Und der Dämon zischt heran

Ein schwarzer Koloß
Über dem Feuermännchen
Grünblau knisternd tanzen

Und das Lichterband
Eine Kette wie Streifen von Gold
Erhellt den alten harschen Schnee

Und ich steh' mit dir am Gleis
Halte fest deine Hand
Deine Hand fest in mir
Warum weinen wir und klammern uns aneinander?

So viele Träume
Zerstörte Illusionen
Kap der Bösen Hoffnung
Die Züge der Nacht machen mich immer traurig

Tschionatulander und Sigune

Rasten auf der Lichtung
Tschionatulander und Sigune
Denken, lieben
Der Geist Gâhmurets
Denken, lieben
Was ist geblieben? Was wird bleiben?

Da läuft der Hund vorbei
Am Hals das kostbare Seil
Sigune liest die Zeichen
Und sie ahnt das Geheimnis

Da reißt der Hund sich los
Sigune sah den Anfang bloß
Tschionatulander, bring' ihn wieder
Fang' den Hund   Ich liebe dich
Hol' das Seil   Liebst Du mich?   Fang' mir den Hund
Bring' es wieder Ich liebe dich   Hol' mir das Seil
Ich liebe dich   Liebst Du mich?   Hol' mir das Seil

Tschionatulander - er bricht auf
Und er wird suchen, lange suchen   Beachte die Wege
Er wird es finden, das Brackenseil   Bleib' auf der Spur
Und dafür sterben
Denken, lieben
Was ist geblieben?
Sigune liest die Zeichen

Wie die Schraube entsteht

Auch Federn pflügten über Papiere
Unter schwedischen Bergen tief in der Erde
Schürfte ein Bergmann nach Erz
Eisenbahner füllten Waggons mit Gestein
Rollten in Gleisen in Richtung Süden
Im Hafen luden Dockarbeiter
Die gierigen Bäuche großer Schiffe
Die unter starker Seeleute Arme
Ächzend durch kalte Meere stampften

Auch Federn pflügten über Papiere
Graue Städte nahmen die Schiffe auf
Emsige Hände löschten die Ladung
Andere löschten mit Löschpapier
Bis das Erz in die Öfen kam
Deren Feuer unlöschbar war
Der Erzbischof hielt eine Predigt
Als Fäuste glühende Klötze walzten
Die fließendes Wasser zum Kochen brachten

Auch Federn pflügten über Papiere
Auf schweren Schleppern trugen Fahrer
Die metallenen Blöcke in den Wind
Geschmolzen gegossen gehämmert gefräst
Gesägt geschliffen und gedreht
Das ist der Weg, wie die Schraube entsteht

Wir verteilten sie im ganzen Land
Wir montierten sie in die Motoren
Wir trieben sie in die Getriebe
Sie brachten Maschinen zum Laufen
Sie brachten Wagen zum Fahren
Sie brachten Panzer zum Rollen

Echofisch

Am Abend laufen die Boote
Heraus aus der schwarzen Bucht
Blick zurück an der Mole stehen
Schnell kleiner werdend Frauen
Stechen, stechen in See
In Richtung des gewölbten Horizonts
Graue Wolkenfetzen jagen
Über das Firmament
Geben manchmal das Licht
Des Mondes frei
Blitz auf dunklen Kronen

Südwester wenden sich nach Nordwest
Sturm peitscht die Wogen auf
Salzwasser in den Pfeifenköpfen
Erstes Eis in Bärten
Dann winden die Männer die Trossen ab
Netze tauchen ein

Und kreuzen
Schweigende Fahrt

Dunst senkt sich
Die schwachen Lichter
Der kleinen Hütten
Auf den Hügeln erlöschen

Der Steuermann schaut zum Stundenglas
Das Boot fährt leicht
Die gleichen Knoten
Stumpfes Starren ins Nichts
Jeder Tag ohne Unterschied
Verschlammte Algen schimmern
In Regenbogenfarben

Bäume hoch
Die Netze sind leer

Nebel steigt
Die Sicht wird frei
Geglättetes Tuch
Kurs auf die Heimatbucht

Keine weißen Möwen
Folgen den stillen Booten
Verklebtes Gefieder treibt im Film
Eine Zeitlang bis es sinkt
Blick nach vorn an der Mole stehen
Schnell größer werdend Kinder
Kehren, kehren zurück
Wie Schlangen fliegen die Taue an Land

Die Brücke und der Fluß

Ein Dröhnen in den Planken
Kalte Winde schütteln den Stahl
Die Träger fest betonverankert
Filigranzeichnung mächtiger Art

Unten reißen die dunklen Fluten
Unbändig an den Werken der Zahl
Unter und über tosen die Wasser
Ungeduldiges Höhnen der Kraft

Das braune Gebräu brodelt unter den Füßen
Ein Ächzen und Stöhnen dringt aus der Tiefe
Es steigt herauf und hämmert sprudelnd
An Halterungen gurgeln Strudel

Gischtspritzer konnten die Balken abweisen
Doch der ständige Schmerz der Erschütterung
Quält das Innere des Gerüstes
In Kabeln und Drähten Hochspannung

Da! Sie bersten, detonieren
Mit Zischen und Knallen zerfetzt sich das Netz
Die feinen Strukturen gehen verloren
Das Gewebe zerbricht, es hält kein Gewicht

Einsame Blicke vom Ufer mit Grausen
Seh'n wie die Fluten
Über das sinkende Machwerk brausen
Sie schließen sich und wie ehedem
Gleitet ruhig der Fluß dahin

Im warmen Wasserturm

Ich war im warmen Wasserturm
Das Licht fiel bräunlich durch die Ritzen
Ich fühlte mich so warm und weich
Durch Löcher sah ich Sonne blitzen

Dann rutschte ich durch schwarze Engen
Glitt gekrümmt ganz ohne Schmerz
Der Tunnel ließ sich nicht bestimmen
Aufgeregt zersprang mein Herz

Dann lag ich nackt an deiner Haut
Viel sanfter als auf Seidenkissen
Ich fragte nicht, ich fühlte nur
War sicher so genug zu wissen

Ich war im warmen Wasserturm
Ich schwebte auf dem Radius
Es gab keinen Hunger, keinen Durst
Keine Forderung, kein Muß

Dann lag ich nackt an deiner Haut
Viel sanfter als auf Seidenkissen
Ich fragte nicht, ich fühlte nur
War sicher so genug zu wissen

Frequent Fliers

Frequent fliers are never scared
Frequent fliers they stay in the air
Never arriving at airports too early
And never too late
And if there's any delay
They patiently take it
As old native hunters
Waiting for their prey

Sometimes you're tempted to believe
That they might look just like you and me
But that's only deceiving in fact they are different
And to be honest: entirely so

Men are likely wearing pinstripe suits
And women wear heavy perfumes
Men are likely wearing elegant coats
And women wear fancy costumes

You can't call them arrogant   They're just the way
That really wouldn't be fair   They are
More precise would be "ignorant"
They don't care who accompanies them in the air

Frequent fliers are never scared
Frequent fliers they stay in the air
Frequent fliers are never scared
When the plane takes off
Just on the runway's last meters

Frequent fliers are never scared
Bumping is fun and they love gusty winds
Frequent fliers are never scared
When an engine quits or the masks drop down
Due to a loss of pressure

They keep on reading their Wall Street Journal
They keep on hammering at their laptop computers
They can't imagine a sudden funeral
In cemetries full of indispensable people
Just as they are themselves
They can't imagine the end of the future

Frequent fliers they stay in the air

Up there

I can see you there
Up in the sky
High above the white clouds
Where the big airplanes fly

Why did you leave me
Tell me why, tell me why
Though you knew how much I loved you
It wasn't fair, it wasn't right
Why did you leave me
Why did you leave me
Please, tell me why

Some said you were something peculiar
I always thought you were something special
Just someone special

Though sometimes you were rough
And treated me badly
I forgive you all of this
I would forgive you even more
If you'd only come back
For just a short while

For a second in close proximity to you
I would give a year of my life or two
Honestly no one, no one but you
Deserved a similar sacrifice

I can see you up there
Return, return, return!

Age of Angst

Age of angst
State of fear
Once safe, now lost
Where do we go from here?

Age of sin
Age of lie
Once we were loud, now we're shy
Once we sang, but now we cry

Age of angst
State of fear
Once safe, now lost
Where do we go from here?

Shunting Engine

From season to season
From year to year
The only thing to change
Is the cracking of my gear

Day after day
Back and forth
Moving alone
On the same short tracks
So many times

I'm pushing and pulling the heavy load
Now dust-covered and torn is my worn-out coat
Once it was shining in clear white-blue
Once I was so strong I could break iron shoes

Day after day
Back and forth
Moving alone
On the same short tracks
So many times

I'm longing for the turntable
My only change, my only movement in life
(That huge turntable larger than life)
But once I turn around
I'm just back to yet another short track

Always quite close to hitting the bumpers
Always quite close to ending my trip
No thruway to see, no light at the end
Of the tunnel I'm stuck in so deep

Was I really supposed to be here
Was that really meant to be my very life
Who pushed me into this forsaken place
Leaving me no chance at all to strive?

For higher achievements
For a track under the sun
Here every yard forward
Is in fact a yard back

Day after day
Back and forth
Moving alone
On the same short tracks
So many times

Let Go

I see myself in a saddle
Bright shiny brown leather
Looking back just for a moment
While whipping slowly from right to left

I see myself relaxed on horseback
Coloured cotton shirt
White shantung hat
Wide bright brim

And there are you, my heart
You're waving
You tried to hold me, to stop me
From constant craving

There you are, my heart
No more yelling and screaming
Now you are silent
Helplessly grieving

Riding the high mountains
Riding the great plains
Heading for the vast open spaces
Heading for the big, blue skies

I see myself in a saddle
Bright shiny brown fur back
Looking back just for a moment
While whipping slowly from right to left

You'll be always in my heart
But I'm leaving
You'll be always in my heart
Don't try any retrieving

You couldn't let go
Couldn't let me go
So I'm leaving now
I'm going, let go

Religious Frenzy

In all of mankind's great beliefs
The gods are no gods of cruelties
They forbid hate, they forbid lies
They say killing locks the door to paradise

In a way all the different gods seem to be
Just like different names for the same idea

How can we be so arrogant
To interpret the will of gods
To know so sure what's right, what's wrong
To tell the goods from the odds
How do we dare to blame our evil deeds on them?

We're living in a state of insanity
We're living in a time of despair
On the brink of a major catastrophe
I can smell the dynamite that hangs in the air

Back to the roots
But back to which?
Back to the dark ages
Where we used to burn a witch?
Without testimony, without evidence
We liked to spike the victim onto a fence
It's no better if we now turn a switch
To a fundament which is not a place for good seed
Because a fundament is made of concrete

For the will to be
For the will to survive
For love and peace
For living with the world in harmony

Racist Frenzy

I closed my eyes and wished myself to a place
Somewhere in this aching world
And in my dream finally
I found what I was always searching for
Black and White, Yellow and Red
Smiling at each other
Working hard together
In a town without hatred

I don't imagine peaceful grazing lambs
But I do believe in peaceful grazing rams
Striving towards a common goal
Relieving of the soul

We're living in a state of insanity
We're living in a time of despair
On the brink of a major catastrophe
I can smell the dynamite that hangs in the air

We used to live as neighbours
We went to the same old school
We played in our backyards
Having fun together was the only rule

Our moms came out to serve cold drinks
Our brothers did the barbeque
It took me some years to realize
How much I had fallen in love with you

As we grew older those things hardly changed
Despite different backgrounds
We remained the same
Until yesterday your father came
And put a bullet through my daddy's brain

Ahh.....
Ahh.....

All of a sudden, out of the blue
A spark ignites the flame
Of hate
That might have ruled amongst us
Centuries ago
Again

Stop it! Stop it!
Stop it! Stop it!

What a madness, what a shame
How can we ever be happy again?

The war of our forefathers
I saw it as a history lesson
My vision was that we learned from their mistakes
To behave in some other way
Eventually

We went fishing, we climbed the mountains, too
We shared each joy and every bruise
Away from this frenzy I hoped we escaped
Until yesterday I heard it was your sister
Who my brother raped

Ahh.....
Ahh.....

All of a sudden, out of the blue
A spark ignites the flame
Of hate
That might have ruled amongst us
Centuries ago
Again

Stop it! Stop it!
Stop it! Stop it!

What a madness, what a shame
How can we ever be happy again?

Twenty-two Black Stretch-Limousines

Twenty-two black stretch-limousines
Another long big one in between
Men in uniform, policebikes
Young and old fur-women scream

They're coming to say their last farewell
They're coming just to show off
And they show off well
Dark sunglasses and coloured hair
It's important what they wear

Twenty-two black stretch-limousines
Another long big one in between
Men in uniform, policebikes
Young and old fur-women scream

He fought hard, and harder he bought
Mansions, blocks, plants and the court
He even bought the church
Whose servants now pray
Though the grievers bend their snaky necks
All his money doesn't bring him back

Twenty-two black stretch-limousines
Another long big one in between
Men in uniform, policebikes
Young and old fur-women scream

All his dirty money won't bring him back

Little Figure Skater

Sliding and gliding
In your tiny white skates
With your neat dark dress
Made of linen and lace
Gently bending your knees
And stretching your legs

Then you go for a jump
And you rise into the air
For a moment you seem to stand still
And so does the mane of your fair hair

Then you land, you glide on
So smooth and yet so strong
Effortlessly hovering
Over invisible tracks
You're dancing pirouettes
And you're flying in triplets

Child, spin around
Spin around while you can
All of my hopes
I'll lay in your hands and feet

Your tiny legs
Your vulnerable small body
Your little heart
Your head so smart

The ice you rule
Is thin and artificial

But you don't know about it
And if you knew you wouldn't want to

And that's alright
With your clear eyes
And your big smile
You will defy the future
And you will break the ice

Skate on, skate away
Skate away while you can
You skate the figures
Don't let the figures skate you
All of my hopes
I'll lay in your hands and feet

Long Shadows

Grey trees leafless
Black birds speechless
Hovering over harsh fields of snow
Under blurring sick-looking skies

By the side of the creek
The shrubs though hard felt so weak
The weary waters decided to freeze
Under a scent of plague brought by a breeze

When the sun was about to get dimmed
The horizon seemed somehow fur-trimmed
Facing the dark with wide open eyes
Afraid of plunging down into an unknown space

Why do I clench my teeth together
Why do I awake with my limbs all numb?
Why do I awake with that pain in my brain
Why do I constantly hear this train in my ear
Tryin' to make me dumb?

Grey hounds soundless
Black ghosts groundless
Hunting down the ancient ravine
Through the long shadows caused
By the full moon beams

With a crack in the ice
The twigs drew back in disguise
The wind started blowing in from the east
And the tumbling fish gathered for the feast

When the moon was about to get dimmed
The horizon seemed somehow fur-trimmed
Facing the dark with wide open eyes
Afraid of plunging down into an unknown space

Why do I clench my teeth together
Why do I awake with my limbs all numb?
Why do I awake with that pain in my brain
Why do I constantly hear this train in my ear
Tryin' to make me dumb?

Coroner's Car

Coroner's car howling through the dark
Leaving behind the screaming hearts
Of those who're left behind and apart

Another unsolved mystery
Another unsolved crime
She's laying in the alley there
But the asphalt turned to thyme

Time for dreaming
Lacked so long
Now it's given plain
Though her tiny virgin soul
Is spilled with maculating stains

Coroner's car howling through the dark
Leaving behind the backsplashed marks
The "Do-not-cross"-line and the bar

Another unsolved mystery
Another unsolved crime
She's fallen in the alley there
But the asphalt turned to thyme

Time for dreaming
Lacked so long
Now it's given plain
Something ventured nothing gained
She took a chance but remained estranged

Fallen angel
Fallen hard
Now raised to the stars
The cushions are prepared for you
Nobody will do you harm anymore

Coroner's car howling through the dark
Through the squalling snow from a single cloud
Eventually it'll be soaked up

Addicted

Addicted to the alarm clock
Addicted to roll call
Addicted to climbing up the hill
And reach the city wall

Addicted to the subway net
Addicted to fine cars
Addicted to the metal stream
That's jammed up to the stars

Addicted to the telephone
Addicted to the desk
Addicted to the setup here
And also to the flash

Addicted to the coffee-shop
Addicted to lunch break
To fancy dishes or fast food
Or simply just cornflakes

Addicted to the media
Addicted to the church
Addicted to the politics
And to creatures that emerge

Addicted to a strong tough man
Addicted to straight course
Addicted to a sharp loud voice
Though it could be quite hoarse

Addicted to the Mother Earth
Addicted to the seas
Addicted to the sun and moon
To everything beyond belief

Addicted to society
Addicted to the bars
Addicted to the dress-up rules
And to coiffeurs from Mars

Addicted to the symphony
A slave to rock'n'roll
Addicted hard to jazz and folk
A slave to rap and soul

Addicted to the galleries
Addicted to wise books
Addicted to the archs and techs
Turned to stone at statues' looks

Addicted to the other sex
Addicted to the same
Addicted both to love and lust
So many times in vain

Addicted to amphetamine
Addicted to cocaine
Addicted to the very gun
That put a bullet through your brain

Mobile Society

We've got nothing to share
No secrets to tell
We were just thrown together
Like beings in hell

We're living in an abandoned world
Estranged from each other we no longer care
Into an abyss of isolation we were hurled
To reach out and approach we can't even dare

And instead of burning fires
Instead of flying sparks
Cold mists soaked our desires
A wall was built between our hearts

Once we lived together
And we worked there where we lived
But because it was the state of the times
We didn't consider that a gift

Nowadays you've got to look
From North to South from East to West
Just to make your living here
You've got to travel far to do your best

And instead of burning fires
Instead of flying sparks
Cold mists soaked our desires
A wall was built between our hearts

Virtual Reality

There's an amusement park
Hidden back in the dark
Of restored factory halls
In the basement of the towers
Of tourist attractions

We put on the masks
We put on the helmets
And we pull down the visors
Though bound to fight
We can't even face each other
We've left the solid ground
And entered a new world
Where everything's only virtually real
We've entered virtual reality

We put on the electronic glove
The steering wheel, the laser sword
And we cruise the unknown oceans
Discovering new worlds
Consisting of data

We're travelling, we're fighting
We survive in virtual reality
Sometimes we're catapulted out
Into a parallel galaxy
We live the solitary life
Of astronauts in space
We live in a singularity
We live in virtual reality

Moving on

I'm moving on the road is clear
Nothing in the world can hold me now
All that seemed to be black is turning blue
It's a new state of mind I'm going through

Out on the freeway big sky's ahead
Leaving all the dark clouds behind my back
The obstacles and thresholds
That once darkened my day
Eventually I passed them by I'm on my way

The hard times I once was fallen on
And the submissions undergone
Don't want to trace the very source no more
Don't want to return to the place I was before

I'm moving on, I'm moving on
The horizon is a-rising
At the end of the tunnel the light turns bright
And the beacon beckons to hold on tight

I'm moving on though the sea might be rough
Nothing in the world can stop me now
All that seemed to be black is turning blue
It's a new state of mind I'm sailing through

Out on the ocean big sky's ahead
Leaving all the humble fish behind astern
The nets and ruses lain out for me
Couldn't stop my course
And were propelled to pieces

I'm moving on, I'm moving on
The horizon is a-rising
I'm moving on, I'm moving on
Leaving all the black shades behind me

All the rude words, all the smashed doors
Broken mirrors and broken promises
I'm moving on, I don't look back
The horizon is a-rising

I'm moving on, the skies are clear
Nothing in the world can hold me now
All that seemed to be black is turning blue
It's a new state of mind I'm flying through

Intolerance

I was thinking about it
I was investigating my soul
For once I set out to be patient and calm
Moderate and tolerant
I was wondering whether I had cancelled my plans

With open hearts and open hands
Open hearts and open hands

And I found out to my very surprise
That I can't close my eyes any longer
When I look around
I see worlds breaking down
Neighbours killing neighbours
Shelling their own towns

I can't bear it
I won't take it
I can't stand it
It's gone too far
Much too far

Intolerance, intolerance
Mushroom clouds over silent waters
Intolerance, intolerance
Explosions set by treaty-breakers
Intolerance, intolerance
Far away from the zone of death
Intolerance, intolerance
Where they can't feel that desperate wrath
Intolerance, intolerance

Stealthy withdrawal from the barren lands
Intolerance, intolerance
Leaving the lost who once welcomed them

With open hearts and open hands
Open hearts and open hands

Intolerance, intolerance
Men dictate to women how to behave
Intolerance, intolerance
They try to lock them up in narrow cells
Intolerance, intolerance
They make them hide their body and their face
Intolerance, intolerance
Shutting them away from the outer world
Intolerance, intolerance
And for their greed to possess them completely
Intolerance, intolerance
They're claiming divine rules

With open hearts and open hands
Open hearts and open hands

I can't bear it
I won't take it
I can't stand it
It's gone too far
Much too far

Intolerance, intolerance
Drunken fathers, silent mothers
Intolerance, intolerance
Take their daughters and sons

On never-ending rides
Intolerance, intolerance
To hurt their souls
For a lifetime
Intolerance, intolerance

With open hearts and open hands
Open hearts and open hands

I can't bear it
I won't take it
I can't stand it
It's gone too far
Much too far

You don't love me anymore

Once there were mountains to be climbed
Once there were seas to be sailed
Farther and farther no boundaries
Seemed to exist for you and me

We went up the hills and sometimes down
Like a king and his queen we wore a crown
Yet without knowing 'cause the crucial things
Only come to your eyes when you can't see them

We walked hand in hand, steadfast and true
Even on rainy days the skies were blue
We thought this state would always go on
We couldn't imagine anything to go wrong

What was it that came between us
How come we didn't realize?
It was a sneaky snail out of Hieronymus' hell
That shot its slow-acting venom into our veins

Now we're sitting paralyzed
Anxiously waiting for the time to pass by
For the death of our emotions to occur
For the peace of the waves that once were so stirred

We let the silence torture our hearts
I feel how I die by hideous arts
But I know my corpse will return to the shore
Though you don't love me anymore

African-American Girl

I met her down on 42nd street
Where she was dancing to the pulsing beat
When she turned around
And looked me straight into the eyes
She was an angel fallen down to me from paradise

Little black beauty, my little black heart
I was falling in love with you right from the start
Little black beauty, my little black soul
You pushed me and you pulled me
Yes, you taught me rock'n'roll

The air was humid and our clothes were all wet
You drew me to a coffee-shop and later to your bed
In your arms so slender and yet so very strong
I forgot just who I was and why I'd come along

Little black beauty, my sweet little heart
I was falling in love with you right from the start
Little black beauty, my little black soul
You pushed me and you pulled me
Yes, you taught me rock'n'roll

The shape of your body
That's pure philosophy
The way you move and kiss
Is absolute extraordinary
You gave me within seconds
All I longed for in my life
You said:"You need it, you deserve it
But I don't want to be your wife!"

Little black beauty, my sweet little heart
I was falling in love with you
And now I'm falling apart
Don't ever leave me, I'm crawling on my knees
Stay with me till kingdom comes
I'm begging darling, please

But now she calls me "traitor"
Though I did nothing wrong
Because she'd seen me in a place
Where she thought I would not belong
Little black beauty, have mercy on me
Without you I feel like a branch
Must feel without a tree

Little black beauty, your jealousy
Pulls me right into a swirl
Little black beauty, my African-American girl
Little black beauty, my sweet little heart
I was falling in love with you
And now I'm falling apart

Feast or Famine

Globetrotting or trodden-down
Food bank or bank account
Day off or lay off
Whooping up or whooping cough

Batoning or feeling the batons
Atom blaze or blazed to atoms
Child porn or pornographed child
Bathing in mud or in soap so mild

Whirling up dust or breathing grit
Littering a highway or adopting it
Polluting the air or having asthma
Sleeping on the floor or on a sofa

Slaughtering or being the swine
Being mediocre or divine
Weighing tons or carrying them
Memorizing or hunting ram

Stemming from God or from the apes
Tasting wine or harvesting grapes
Frozen yoghurt or frozen feet
Beaten up or dance to the beat

Living in a shell or being shelled
Being risen or having knelt
Literature professor or illiterate
Executive or execution writ

Being licensed or having lice
Charter flights or flies in the eyes
Obedient servant or domina
Working topless or wearing a bra

On a palm beach or in a small cell
Paradise breeze or freeze in hell
New poverty or austerity
Old misery or prosperity

Gold credit card or no credit at all
Call of the wild or the last call
Lavish tables or empty plates
Giving no aid or having AIDS

Compact car or stretched limousine
All you can eat or lean cuisine
Cardiac disease or Cadillac lease
Worn-out clothes or Golden Fleece

Dumping or living on the dump
Building a bridge or doing the jump
Watching waves or drowning in the flood
Pod of whales or whale in the pot

Being deaf or trying to scream
Giant Mines or dwarf in the seam
Throwing a blinker or biting on it
Calculating or without any wit

Drilling a hole or being the board
Open the heart or erecting a fort
Smiling torturer or tortured smile
Teased every day or once in a while

Riding a horse or taken for a ride
Fight for fuel or fuelled fight
Nightmare or a knight on a mare
Moonshadow or solar flare

Large as life or being at large
Charging after or being charged
Open ranch or at close range
Looking familiar or seeming strange

Top rank or first in the row
Wine and cheese or milking the cow
Four-poster-bed or straw mattress
Empress or a court mistress

Eating a dish or washing it
Chewing it all or just a bit
Burned by the sun or sunkist
Orthodox or atheist

Cordon bleu or police cordon
Nature park or concrete garden
Making a curbstone or working on it
Sitting on a bowl or smoking shit

Dole bananas or living on the dole
Factory trawlers or boat in the mole
Yellowbelly or yellow liver
Dying brave or exposed to a shiver

Just had to

Just had another call to answer
Just had to sign another deal
Just had to write another letter
Just had to make another client feel better

Just had to make a hotel reservation
Just had to book another flight
Just had to establish a new connection
Just had to make it to my boss' satisfaction

Just had to prepare a conference paper
Just had to write a moving speech
Just had to give a short interview
Just had to run for a dark blue suit

Just had to visit my old dentist
Just had to go to my car dealership
Just had to appear at a business luncheon
Just felt worse there than in the London dungeon

Just had to tell my wife I'll be late
Just had to cancel the meeting with my friends
Just had to put some stamps on the packet
Just had to fix my tennis racket

Just had to take my kids to school
Just had to pick them up for the pool
Just had to remember how you kissed
Just had to think of how much we missed

Just had to withstand another temptation
Just had to better plan my recreation
Just had to go to the shopping mall
Just had to attend my own funeral

Anxiety Attack

Waking up in the middle of the night
To an image of a bad dream scene
So deeply disturbing I do not dare to breathe
Hatschepsut had opened false doors for me

Creeping and crawling up from the inner darkness
An evil power gets hold of me
I am submitted to an oppressive yoke
But still I cannot pull the heavy load

I'm moving all too fast these days
I don't know how to stop
Or how to change my ways
I'm so scared and so hurt inside
The pain goes on while I close my eyes

Something is coming slowly
But I'm nailed to my bed
Approaching me directly taking no detour
Screaming loud and clearly
But my voice can't be heard
I'm choking and I shiver in the agony of fear

The vast abundance of unlimited space
Is shrinking to a frightening void
I'm afraid of imploding like a super-nova
I wish myself to a place far far away

I'm moving all too fast these days
I don't know how to stop
Or how to change my ways
I'm so scared and so hurt inside
The pain goes on while I close my eyes

Help me someone, lay healing hands on me
I cannot go on like this anymore
I'm stuck in the middle, I breathe but I sputter
Hatschepsut has opened false doors for me

Verge of Collapse

The people and the country
Where I was raised when I was young
Appear so strange to me today
As if they were a lie

My friends who used to play with me
Are sluggish now and old
Broadened fields and clear-cut woods
Even the river doesn't flow
The way he always did
A hole is in the upper sky
And the weather's changed
This unhappiness of mine remains for sure untold
Thinking back to gracious days
That are lost like a strike
To the sea forever and for good

Everywhere I look around
No happy people to be found
How pitiful young folks behave
Who were considered the hope of the future
Dancing, singing, laughter too
Is dying on the way

How we were poisoned with sweet things
In honey floats the gall
The outside world looks beautiful
Blooming in white and green and red
The inner colour's changed
And has become as dark as death
All that are seduced by her
Should flee the evil spell
With harnesses and helmets bright
Push from the shore and cross
The sea no longer sorrowful

Ready when you are

Relax, relax, relax
Take a deep breath
You've worked so hard
For this moment
You endured so much
You've been so hard on yourself

Now the time has come
To bring in the harvest
The grapes are full and ripe
You really did your best
And it's your turn now
You can be anxious
But no longer scared

We're ready when you are
We're ready when you are

Relax, relax, relax
You are well prepared
You took so much care
You've been trained excellently
And you're equipped so well
You won't shy back now

We're ready when you are
We're ready when you are

Now get into the left seat
Take over the controls
Apply maximum throttle
And you will be lifted up
Just give us the signal
And we let you go

We're ready when you are
We're ready when you are

Mein Schmerz und Ich

Mein Schmerz und ich
Wir haben eine seltsame Beziehung
Wir kennen uns schon lang
Ganz viele Jahre
Ich weiß nicht, wie viele

Ich bin niemals allein
Wir haben ein ganz besonderes Verhältnis
Als könnt' der eine nicht ohne den anderen sein
Er kennt mich so gut
Er wartet auf mich und weiß wann ich komm'

Und in der Nacht
Lieg' ich wach in Angst und Erwartung
Er ist bei mir
Er sagt: Ich bin da wie ein Freund
Doch ich weine

Mein Schmerz und ich
Wir haben eine seltsame Beziehung
Wir kennen uns schon lang
Ganz viele Jahre
Ich weiß nicht, wie viele

Er weicht nicht von meiner Seite
Wir kennen uns so gut
War ich jemals allein?
Doch genau das möcht' ich jetzt sein
Ich sag: Auf Wiedersehen
Zu meinem Schmerz
Wie zu einem alten Freund
Der mich über die Zeit
Durch seine Nähe tief verletzt hat

Ich laß' ihn im Regen stehn
Und für mich selbst
Ist es an der Zeit zu gehn
Ich bin frei

Strg + Alt + Entf

Neulich hatte mein Computer
Mal wieder ein Problem
Fand keine Dateien
Die Pfade waren inkorrekt
Zugriffe auf Bibliotheken
Wurden verweigert
Schließlich fror er ein
Stand kalt und still

Draußen war es grau
Ein wolkenverhangener Tag
Leise fiel ein kühler Regen
Herbst

Wie so oft griff ich jetzt
Zum Mittel des letzten Versuchs
Ich drückte gleichzeitig
Strg + Alt + Entf

Da geschah etwas überaus Merkwürdiges
Mir wurde ganz leicht ums Herz
Als würde ich schweben
Ach was, würd' ich, ich schwebte

Ich weiß nicht wo ich war
Aber irgendwo im Zimmer
Der Bildschirm flackerte
Leuchtete bunt
Und der Stuhl davor war leer

Strg + Alt + Entf

Es ist so schön
Ich bin nicht mehr da
Doch kann alles noch sehen
Die virtuellen Welten und die realen
Bereiten sich gegenseitig
Nunmehr keine Qualen

Der Bildschirm flackert
Leuchtet bunt
Und der Stuhl davor ist leer

Strg + Alt + Entf

Mit Dir und in Dir

Deine
Seidigen Haare
Und deine
Blauen Augen

Deine
Sanfte Stimme
Dein Atem
Eine Sommerbrise

Ich möchte bei Dir sein
Für immer und einen Tag
Möchte mich Dir anvertrau'n
Möchte mich trau'n
Mit Dir

Deine
Samtigen Lippen
Und deine
Weiche Haut

Deine
Schlanken Arme
Und deine
Zarten Hände

Ich möchte in Dir versinken
Möchte in Dir ertrinken
Möchte mich Dir geben
Bis ich mich selbst
Nicht mehr spür'

Andere

Andere sind schneller
Andere sind größer
Andere sind heller
Als ich

Andere fahr'n teure Wagen
Tragen feinen Stoff
Und blütenweiße Kragen
Ich nicht

Andere sind Häuserbauer
Andere haben Geld
Und dazu auch sehr viel Power
Ich nicht

Andere stählen ihren Körper
Essen nur Salat
Trinken Selters in der Lobby
Ich nicht

Anders als die andern
Entsprech' ich keinem Ideal
Anders als die andern
Und doch ganz normal
Oder etwa nicht?

Mein Wissen ist nur angelesen

Mein Wissen ist nur angelesen
Von der Welt hab' ich nicht viel gesehen
Und das bißchen, das ich kenne
Find' ich auch überhaupt nicht schön

Mein Wissen ist nur angelesen
Doch bin ich auch mal im Kino gewesen
Meine Wirklichkeit, die ist nur zweiter Hand
Gebraucht, recycelt und dann wieder verbrannt

Mein Wissen ist nur angelesen
Ich surfe auf dem Internet
Immer mit dem Hirn am Schirm
Im schmalen Zimmer mit dem kleinen Bett

Mein Wissen ist nur angelesen
Politikerreden hab' ich gespeichert
Dokumentkopien von Entwicklungen
Bildertafeln von Elementen

Mein Wissen ist nur angelesen
Selbst weitergelesen hab' ich nicht
Ich habe Angst, die Wahrheit zu erleben
Alles Echte macht mir Angst

Ich fürchte mich vor zärtlichen Händen
Und vor Küssen, den feuchten, erst recht
Meine Bücher halten Abstand
Und der Rechner hält sich mit Anstand zurück

The Black T-Shirt

Rockstars cool in the Carlton
And hot on stage in the nights
Curvy girls, Rodeo Drive
Pimped up cars with neon lights

I don't need a lot
To be in the center stage
I can distinguish myself from
And still be a part of the rest
And that feels good, oh yeah

I can smoke a cigarette
I can proudly admit I quit
I can hold on to my whisky glass
I can sip from my still water cup
And that feels good, oh yeah

Mercenaries in the jungle
Marshals sheltering the skies
Ray Bans in the desert land
High above the vulture flies

I don't need a lot
To be in the center stage
I can distinguish myself from
And still be a part of the rest
And that feels good, oh yeah

I can smoke a cigarette
I can proudly admit I quit
I can hold on to my whisky glass
I can sip from my still water cup
And that feels good, oh yeah

Terrorists hoping they're martyrs
Longing for their paradise
God is great but he doesn't let them in
For the pain they caused on Earth

I don't need a lot
To be in the center stage
I can distinguish myself from
And still be a part of the rest
And that feels good, oh yeah

I can smoke a cigarette
I can proudly admit I quit
I can hold on to my whisky glass
I can sip from my still water cup
And that feels good, oh yeah

If I come from Brooklyn
Or if I am from Dublin
If I sit in a bar in Berlin
Pay in Euro, Bucks, Pound Sterling

I don't need a lot
To be in the center stage
I can distinguish myself from
And still be a part of the rest
And that feels good, oh yeah

I put my black T-Shirt on
And that feels good, oh yeah
It fits so tight I really
Have to watch my line
I collect the feverish glances
Of the pretty girls around
And I'm seeing in the eyes
Of the guys on the floor
Either adornment or despise
Depending on the course
For which they set their sail

And that feels good, oh yeah

When you ain't got a friend

You say it is cold outside
From the colored sky
You tell a storm is moving in
It is too silent in the house
The rooms are lit by recessed light
Every creak you can hear
Will make you shriek
You say you won't make it
Through the night

When you ain't got a friend
You feel the space is being bent
When you ain't got a friend
You're losing track of everything
When you're alone
Your head becomes heavy as a stone

You had a rough life as a child
Your daddy left you
So your mom put up the fight
When she got too weak at times
You had to jump into the wild
The load seemed too high
And you started to cry
You thought you wouldn't make it
Through the night

When you ain't got a friend
You feel the space is being bent
When you ain't got a friend
You're losing track of everything
When you're alone
Your head becomes heavy as a stone

I will offer to you
What no scientist can do
A freaky ride on a ray of light
Let me be your lover
But not only for tonight
And I will double
The speed of light
For you

Cold Spring Rain

Come on down, cold spring rain
And wash away my pain
Wash away my sorrow
Wash off of me the sin and the lie
Please wash away my shame, oh no

I'm not sure what really has been my crime
I just fell in love once upon a time
With a girl, dark hair and far away eyes
Her laughter rang like paradise
And made me a silent pantomime

We sat in a bar and talked all night
We were excited but
There was the fear and the fright
We held our hands, glanced at each other
This moment there was no more sister and brother
We felt so strange but it felt alright

We parted with the rise of the sun
Before even starting the real fun
Accompanying you would have been a mistake
But letting you go was even worse

A station somewhere in this clueless city
You walked your bicycle from a train
I saw you again, but you didn't see me
I was scared to shout and that was the pity
The chance of a lifetime was given to me twice
I failed, I failed, I failed, I failed
I failed and lost your paradise

Ich dringe in Dich

Ich dringe in Dich
In dein Innerstes
Da wo es rot ist
Und warm
Und fleischig
Da wo es weh tut
Da wo es gut tut

Ich dringe in Dich
In dein Innerstes
Da wo es grau ist
Und schnecken-schleimig
Da wo es weh tut
Und nicht mehr gut tut

Ich dringe in Dich
In dein Innerstes
Tief, tief
Du jauchzt
Du schreist
Du lachst
Du weinst

Du ziehst mich in Dich
Du stößt mich aus Dir
Dein Leid ist Freude
Die Lust dein Schmerz

Ich dringe in Dich
In dein Innerstes
Du willst es so

Fasan

Am falschen Ort zur falschen Zeit
Und das dein Leben lang
Man hat dich entwurzelt
In dies Land gebracht
Schon vor langer Zeit

Du kannst dich nicht erinnern wie es war
In einer Heimat, die nicht deine war
Und in dem Land, wo Du jetzt lebst
So sehr Du dich mühst
Und nach was Du auch strebst
Wirst Du immer ein Fremder sein

Selbst wenn Du felsenfest glaubst
Du paßt hier rein
Wirst Du doch immer anders sein
Die Art wie Du stehst
Und die Art wie Du gehst
Die Art wie Du fliegst
Und deinen Kopf drehst

Deine Federn passen nicht zum Terrain
Deine Laute sind nur sehr schwer zu verstehen
Du hast keine Tarnung
Bist von jedem zu erspähen
Insbesondere von den Jägern
Die mit ihren Flinten
Bereits im Anschlag stehen

Der schlechte Rat ist
Du solltest wirklich gehen
Doch Du weißt nicht wohin
Und ich weiß es auch nicht
Armer Fasan
Armes Schwein

Ex und Hopp

Ex-Ministerin
Ex-Geliebter
Echse
Excel-Tabelle
Ex-Vertriebener

Ex und Hopp

In der Bar
Sie stellt mir den Drink hin
Hochprozentig
Ich will nicht, doch ich muß

Alle schauen mich an
Los runter damit
Ex und Hopp

Ich denk' an mein Leben
So mißraten
Keine Lehrstelle
Eine Leerstelle
Im System
Doch was soll's?
Ex und Hopp

Sie will nur Sex
Sex und Hopp
Ich bin doch kein Bunny
Ich will doch Liebe
In deinen Armen sein
Und nicht vergessen

Kein Bums für eine Nacht
Kein Ex und Hopp

Sex und Hopp
Ex und Hopp
Okay, gib' mir den Drink...

Kleiner Pilot

Kleiner Pilot
Nimm' mich mit auf die Reise
Halt mich fest an der Hand
Wenn ich einsteige
In Deine bunte Maschine

Wir rollen auf der Startbahn
Schneller und schneller
Bis wir schließlich abheben
Und endlich schweben
Wie ein stolzer Vogel

Kleiner Pilot
Nimm' mich mit auf die Reise
Flieg' mit mir durch die Nacht
Über uns ein Meer von Sternen
Und unter uns gleiten
Dahin Feld und Stadt

Ich drück' meine Nase
Dicht an die Scheibe
Und durch meinen Atem
Beschlägt leicht das Glas

Die Motoren summen
Ich werde ganz müde
Wenn Du nichts erzählst
Fall ich in den Schlaf

Wolkengesicht

Du schwebst heran
Fratze aus dem All
Vor dunkelblauem Nachthimmel
Ein Stern als Pupille
Das Auge zerfließt

Mein Herz ist zerrissen
Warum bist Du zurück?
Dein Blick verfolgt mich
Dein warmer Atem
Deine wallenden Haare
Deine wogenden Brüste
Riechen nach Meer

Ich spür' den Druck
Als Du mich umfängst
Deine Hände
Halten die meinen
Sie streichen über
Mein müdes Gesicht

Du machst mich jung
Nicht weil Du jung bist
Da lodert ein Feuer
Es hat mich schon erfaßt
Wolkengesicht

Lichtgestalt

Meine neuen Gedanken
Sind gar nicht neu
Sie war'n schon mal da
Jetzt sind sie zurück
Wie eine Fata Morgana

Ich liebte Dich
Das ist lange her
Du wußtest es und hast
Mit mir gespielt
Erst als ich mich anders entschied
Wolltest Du Dich ganz geben

Doch da war ich schon zu fern
Jahre, viele Jahre sind vergangen
Lichtgestalt
Ich erinnere mich, ich denke an Dich
Wo warst Du, warum hörte ich nichts?

In meinen Träumen umfaßte ich Dich
Sanftest, doch immer fester
Wie der Kegel die Lava umschließt
Bis er birst
Und dann feurig in den Nachthimmel spritzt

Ich will Dich wieder sehen
Um den Preis, daß Du grau bist
Um den Preis von Falten
Um den Preis von Brüsten
Die durch das Gewicht der Jahre
Nicht mehr voll sind
Aber doch ein stilles Blühen haben
Wie die Gärten der Semiramis

Ich würde Deinen Körper
Immer noch lieben
Ein wildes Flötenspiel
Kommt mir in den Sinn
Wir blasen bis zur Erschöpfung
Bis zur Eruption der höchsten
Und schönsten Töne

Ich fantasiere
Denn ich habe Dich nicht gefunden
Noch bin ich auf der Suche
Irgendwo da draußen
Mußt Du sein
Doch ich werde Dich finden
Des sei Dir gewiß!!!

Sternschnuppe

Ich war wach
Bis tief in die Nacht
Ich trank Rotwein
Mein Hals war warm
Mein Zunge ein Pelz
Ich starrte hinaus
In den dunklen Himmel
In dem verhalten
Unzählige Lichter funkelten
Glühwürmchen festgenagelt
Millionen von Jahren
Vielleicht schon tot

Doch noch immer fliegt das Licht
Alles ist still
Nur von fern eine Bahn
Ein schmaler Bogen leuchtet
Auf dem Rücken der Berge
Fast erstickt vom schwarzen Raum

Da stürzt ein Stern
Wie aus dem Nichts
Er wußte es wohl selber nicht
Ahnte es auch nicht vor tausend Jahren
Eine Kupferkugel schießt
Herunter und herab

Ein Sekundenbruchteil
Eigentlich zu kurz
Für die majestätische Größe im Aufflackern
Direkt vorm Vergehen

Man sagt, ich muß mir jetzt
Was wünschen
Doch mein Atem stockt
Ich fange an zu friern
Der gefallene Stern
Er fiel allein

Feuergeist

Du kommst flüssig und brennend
In mein zerrissenes Herz
Fließt in das wunde rohe Fleisch
Deine Mähne weht rassig wild

Ein blauer Kristall
Ein goldenes Band
Schreit: Lebe stark
An den langen kräftigen Fingern
Drei Zacken hat der Königsring

Komm' ich oder Du?
Du saugst mich an
Und ich verzehr' mich nach Dir

Der letzte Wagen
Ist gerade gefahren
Die stählerne Stange
An den Rücken gepreßt

Wir stehen und warten
Der Wind ist kalt
Wir streicheln unsere Wangen
Und halten unsere Hände
Sind eng umschlungen
Die Zeit steht still

Mit dem ersten Zug
Des neuen Tags
Laß' ich Dich los
Ich bin wie geschlagen